Pound a
Poem

Pound a
Poem

The winning entries from the UK
schools poetry competition

metro

Published by Metro Publishing
an imprint of John Blake Publishing Ltd
3 Bramber Court, 2 Bramber Road,
London W14 9PB, England

www.johnblakepublishing.co.uk

First published in hardback in 2009

ISBN: 978-1-84454-833-0

British Library Cataloguing-in-Publication Data:

A catalogue record for this book is available from the British Library.

Design by www.envydesign.co.uk

Printed in the UK by CPI William Clowes, Beccles NR34 7TL

1 3 5 7 9 10 8 6 4 2

Illustrations by Myrna Sayers

Photographs on pages 6, 14, 22, 82, 104, 108, 124, 128, 138, 158, 174, 178, 192 and 208
reproduced courtesy of Rex Features; photograph on page 96 reproduced courtesy of
Vincent Connare; all other photographs supplied by celebrity poets and endorsers.

Papers used by John Blake Publishing are natural,
recyclable products made from wood grown in sustainable forests.
The manufacturing processes conform to the environmental
regulations of the country of origin.

Pound a Poem is proudly sponsored by

Rays of Sunshine

There's a Ray of Sunshine
That casts its beam
And helps to fulfil these children's dream
They make a wish which they hope will come true
And Rays of Sunshine do what they do
They create the ways to grant these wishes
It can be meeting someone famous
Or swimming with the fishes
It can be a lifetime holiday
Or something obscure
Whatever the wish
It's part of the cure
For these little people to
To have their dream, come alive
With laughter and fun, scope and drive
Rays of Sunshine make it happen,
So that families can participate
Enjoy the moments and appreciate
Those memories that they all will cherish and savour
Of that special time, so they can forever taste the flavour
Of the excitement that these children receive
In trusting that they can believe
That life can be both generous and kind
And that there is a little happiness they can find.
This book is dedicated to all those brave children
Who have enjoyed their special time with the
Rays of Sunshine team
And been a part of Rays of Sunshine's dream!

A Word About Pound a Poem

In 2005, Celia Abrahams, a dedicated charity fundraiser, had an idea to do some fundraising around one of her loves – poetry. Celia gradually formed around her a team of volunteers, all experts in their field, and together they built the concept. The team wanted to craft something that would help teach children about the importance of healthy eating and just how vital it is that we all try and eat five potions of fruit and vegetables every day. Poetry had always been at the heart of the concept and so it was decided that children would be asked to write a poem about fruit and vegetables; it was also a fantastic way of further engaging children with literacy. At the same time, the team wanted the children involved to recognise that they had the potential to help other children who are living with life threatening illnesses and so Pound a Poem was born. Children were asked to pay £1 for every poem they entered into the competition. All of that money has been used specifically by Rays of Sunshine Children's Charity, to grant wishes for terminally and seriously ill children across the UK.

Pound a Poem is now enjoying its second year and has been hugely successful. We are proud to have had support from so many wonderful people and organisations, all listed in our acknowledgments, without whom we would have not been able to achieve such success.

We would like to thank all the schools that engaged with Pound a Poem 2008/2009. Congratulations to everyone that entered a poem into this year's competition. They were all wonderful. Thanks you for raising vital funds for Rays of Sunshine.

On behalf of the Rays of Sunshine Children's Charity and the children we help; and from our Trustees, supporters and volunteers, a very big thank you to Celia and the team for your passion and enthusiasm that made it all happen.

Acknowledgements

Thank you ...

So many people have been involved with Pound a Poem since its inception. We are incredibly grateful to you all. Without you, we would not be where we are today. Pound a Poem and Rays of Sunshine would like to thank you for support and for giving so much commitment and enthusiasm.

We would like to thank the following for their support and expertise:

Barbados Tourist Board
Bolton Wanderers Football Club
British Airways
Cecil Rosen Foundation
Costco
Darcey Bussell
Department for Education and Skills
Education Direct
Espresso
Everyclick.com
Gordon Ramsay
Impact, Design and Marketing
Isbi Schools
JazzyMedia Ltd

John Blake Publishing
Landsbanki
Leona Lewis
Moving Picture Company
National Literacy Trust
North Agency
Poetry Society
Royal Society of Medicine
Scholastic Publishing UK
The Rt Hon David Cameron MP
The Rt Hon Gordon Brown MP
The Rt Hon Margaret Hodge MBE MP
Theo Walcott
The Sobell Foundation

We would also like to thank all the poets for their encouragement and participation.

To the Production Team, who have been such a driving force behind Pound a Poem:

Adam Abrahams
Andrew Feldman
Ann Miller
Anthony Abrahams
Barrie Tankel
Celia Abrahams
Debbie Carne
Edward Kerner
Geraldine Kreiger
Jayne Franklin
Judy Dewinter
Karen Harris
Katie Lester
Katy Abrahams
Kim Britten
Laura Nathan

Lisa Ronson
Mark Abrahams
Michael Abrahams
Michael Mowlem
Myrna Sayers
Nikki Woolf
Paul Corren
Penny Telfer
Richard Phillips
Ruth Abrahams
Ruth Mowlem
Susannah Price
Dan Freedman
Talia Jordan
Paul Summerfield

Finally, huge thanks to all the judges in the competition who had the most enjoyable, but also the most difficult job of reading all the poems and deciding the winners. Thank you for your valuable time.

Acknowledgement to Celia Abrahams

These acknowledgments would not be complete without saying a few words about the creator of Pound a Poem. Celia Abrahams, along with her cousin Richard Phillips, came up with the wonderful idea of Pound a Poem. Not only is Pound a Poem a fantastic fundraising initiative which raises money for charity, but it also encourages children's understanding of poetry, literacy and healthy eating. With three children and nine grandchildren of her own, Celia understands how important it is to nurture and educate today's youth.

Celia's vision, hard work and sheer determination has seen Pound a Poem grow from just a great idea to a fully-fledged national competition with the support of Prime Ministers, renowned poets and authors as well as today's most loved celebrities. Celia's abilities as a fundraiser are second to none; she inspires and excites everyone she meets. Even in the face of adversity, Celia has never faltered and continues working selflessly for charity. She is a pleasure to work with and a truly remarkable person.

Congratulations Celia, on all you have achieved and on the continued success of Pound a Poem.

10 DOWNING STREET
LONDON SW1A 2AA

THE PRIME MINISTER

I am delighted to give my personal backing to the Pound a Poem competition, in aid of Rays of Sunshine Children's Charity. This fantastic initiative for school children aged 5-11 promotes literacy, healthy eating and good citizenship.

It is particularly relevant this year given that 2008 is the national Year of Reading. By participating, children will be able to learn more about poetry whilst also helping children less fortunate than themselves by raising funds for Rays of Sunshine which grants wishes for terminally and seriously ill children across the UK.

So my congratulations to everyone involved with Pound a Poem, particularly the schools and the children taking part. It's a great idea and deserves continued widespread support.

Best wishes,

Gordon Brown

June 2008

Rt Hon DAVID CAMERON MP

HOUSE OF COMMONS
LONDON SW1A 0AA

LEADER OF THE OPPOSITION

September 2008

"Pound a Poem"

I am delighted to send my best wishes to everyone participating in this year's competition, in support of Rays of Sunshine.

Rays of Sunshine has made a huge difference to the lives of many children and their families. We can see from the Rays of Sunshine video just how much it means when children's dreams are turned into reality. It has also provided vitally needed equipment, and many have cause to be grateful for all it has achieved.

So this is a great choice of charity for this year's "Pound a Poem" competition. Last year's competition was a real success. I am sure it has inspired more young poets to put pen to paper this year, and that this collection will once again amuse and stir the imagination.

I would like to congratulate everyone involved in the 2008 competition - and to wish good luck to all those who are entering.

David Cameron

Gordon Ramsay, Celebrity Chef

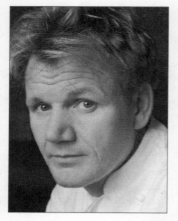

'As a Patron of Rays of Sunshine Children's Charity I am thrilled to support Pound a Poem 2008. This competition not only inspires children to be more creative, but more creative with food, and all whilst raising money for Rays of Sunshine – a wonderful charity which grants wishes for terminally and seriously ill children across the UK.'

Leona Lewis, Singer

'I am so proud to support Pound a Poem 2008, I work closely with Rays of Sunshine and the work they do is amazing in making so many dreams come true!'

Darcey Bussell CBE, Prima Ballerina

'I'm so pleased to be able to support Pound a Poem again this year. Pound a poem is a wonderful concept and I'm sure your poems about fruit and vegetables are brilliant!'

Theo Walcott, Arsenal and England Striker

'Pound a Poem is a great idea! All your poems will make dreams come true for some very special children.'

The Poems

Can I Eat You?

Can I eat you?
Lovely and sweet
Especially juicy
My favourite
Especially juicy
No better fruit
Tasty and sweet
In my tummy
Now I'm happy
Especially juicy

Jacob Alexandrou • Year 1
St Gerrards Junior School
Wales

Fruit and Vegetables

Green pears are very juicy
Delicious, yummy, goody, goody, goody
Oranges are very tasty
With lots of pips inside

I don't like bananas
I don't know why.
Tomatoes are absolutely yucky
Because they make me cry

I love cucumbers
And carrots too
They go crunch, crunch, crunch
Inside your mouth
How about you?

Eliza Mackworth-Prael • Year 1
The Abbey Junior School
Reading

Fruit is Great

Fruit is great
I love to eat strawberries, my favourite

Red juicy apples I eat for my lunch
Yum yum, munch munch

You need to eat fruit as it is good for you
Oranges, pears, bananas are my favourite too

It makes me healthy, fit and strong
It helps my body grow long and long

The fruit can also make yummy things
Like smoothies with pineapple rings

Milan Milovic • Year 1
St Mary's R C Primary School
Manchester

Lord Alan Sugar
Business Entrepreneur

The Pressure Cooker

Sugar snap peas masquerading as soya beans,

Talentless tofu can't compete with aubergine,

Put them all in a pressure cooker,

And if they can't take the heat, get them out of the kitchen!

Golden Corn

Golden Corn waves in the Autumn breeze,

Blowing everywhere you will find lots of seeds,

It's going to be picked in a few days time,

There is frost on the frozen ground.

Emily Bauer • Year 1
Hunter Hall School
Cumbria

Grapes Are Green

Grapes are green
And so is a bean.

I love cherries
I love berries.

Apples are green and red
They are good for me the dentist said.

Romany Ryan • Year 1
Whittington Primary School
Staffordshire

Harvest Baskets

In my harvest basket I can see ...
Wife wheat,
Crunchy carrots,
Sharp strawberries,
Crisp cabbages,
Lovely leeks,
Bumpy broccoli.

Thomas Hawkins • Year 1
Tadley School
Hampshire

Wendy Cope

Poet

The Orange

At lunchtime I bought a huge orange –
The size of it made us all laugh.
I peeled and shared it with Robert and Dave –
They got quarters and I had a half.

And that orange, it made me so happy,
As ordinary things often do
Just lately. The shopping. A walk in the park.
This is peace and contentment. It's new.

The rest of the day was quite easy.
I did all the jobs on my list
And enjoyed them and had some time over.
I love you. I'm glad I exist.

This poem is from
Wendy Cope's book
**Two Cures for Love:
Selected Poems**,
published by Faber.
Appears with the
author's permission.

11

I Love School Jackets

I like:

Green broccoli 'trees',
Red apples for munching at break,
Grapes that I put in my mouth to make chipmunk cheeks,
Tomatoes, because they squirt,
Oranges……but not the stringy bits,
Cucumber, because it is juicy,
And peas to chase on my plate.

But best of all I LOVE school jacket potato for my lunch.

It's Yummy.

Ellen Chancellor • Year 1
Redland High School
Bristol

I See

I see red, strawberry sweet and squeezy
I see yellow, pepper disgusting and has pips in
I see blue, blueberries sour and juicy
I see green, broccoli watery and dotty
I see orange, orange juicy and sweet
I see purple, cabbage crunchy and big
I see brown, kiwi soft and hairy

Ben Webster • Year 1
The Elms Primary School
Nottingham

Alan Bennett

Playwright

Doubts about Sprouts

I have my doubts about sprouts
And make scenes over beans
What I really enjoy
Is a big green savoy

(With bacon and chestnut and cream)

My Poem

Carrots are my favourite,
Sweetcorn I adore,
When my mummy cooks it for my tea,
I always ask for more.

Ella Margetts • Year 1
St John's C E Primary School
Essex

My Veg Poem

Lettuce and cabbage and all the green things,
Grow in the fields where the birds like to sing.

The birds live in trees and have worms for their tea.

But lettuce and cabbage are better for me.

Ross Crawford • Year 1
Carleith Primary School
Scotland

James Nesbitt
Actor

From Ulster

From Ulster, adrift, I increasingly turn to the symbols that bring home home
Antrim's green glens, The Auld Lammas Fair, Heaney's da digging the loam
But Ireland to me means the spud, the tattie, that knotted oval of joy
Boiled, roasted or mashed with butter and salt, my comfort, my saviour, my boy.

Peas Please

Pick peas,
Eat peas,
All gone,
Some more please!

Hugh Holland Craven • Year 1
St Mary Magdalen's Catholic School
London

Plum and Pear

I love my mum,
She always buys me a purple plum,
Which tastes yum yum
When it's in my tum tum.

Whenever I eat a juicy pear,
I have to take care,
Because people always stare
When it gets stuck in my hair.

Jessica Sheldon • Year 1
St Paul's Catholic Primary School
Cheshire

Vegetables

Vegetables grow in the ground,
The farmers grow them all around.

In garden everywhere they do flourish,
And when we eat them, they do nourish.

Connie Biccock • Year 1
Holbeach Primary School
Lincolnshire

Jonathan Ross

Television Presenter

Of all the fruit I've ever tasted

Of all the fruit I've ever tasted
Swallowed down and never wasted
The one that I'm the biggest fan of
Is the tasty, curvy, sweet bananof.
On their own or in a bunch
Nothing beats 'em with your lunch
Soft and scrummy taste nirvana
That's my fave, divine birnana

Ready wrapped but quick to open
Every meal time I'd be hopin'
That after cheese and pickle sarnie
My mum would offer ripe banarny

We share with apes some DNA
A certain look, a love of play
The records by the man Santana
And both adore to eat bantana

There is one thing that leaves me miffed
With Mother Nature's yellow gift
And that is just the name – banana
It's very, very difficult to find words that rhyme with it.

The Vegetable Race

And they're off.....
The cucumber cart wheeled slowly,
Tumbled over the turnip and leaps over the leeks,
She bounced over the brussel,
And tiptoed past the tomato,
Hooray the cucumber is the winner!

Olivia Rushton • Year 1
Hadley Wood Primary School
Barnet

Anna Maxted

Poet

Unmentionable Vegetables

I despair
at the sight of an avocado pear.
I regret
being offered courgette.
I scorn
sweetcorn.
One sniff of a pea
I flee.
You could stamp and shout,
I will not eat a sprout.
You could roar and shriek
I refuse to taste a leek.
If I spy a mushroom
I rush from the room.
Let us
not even speak of lettuce.
So it's funny
that any supper made by Mummy
is the height of yummy.
I scrape the plate to discover

she's used the sauce to cover
about a million unmentionable
vegetables.
That blender lets her hide
just about anything inside
a chicken stew, or a meat or cheese sauce.
It's outrageous dinner dishonesty of course.
She disguises every green thing so I'm not suspicious.
I'll never admit it – they're all delicious.

Apple

Appetising and crunchy,
Pleasing to eat,
Pale inside,
Lovely and juicy,
Every apple tastes of the blue sky.

Josie Lee • Year 2
R L Hughes Primary School
Wigan

Carrots

Parrots eat carrots
They eat them all the time
Sometimes they are crunchy
And I think that is fine

You can cook them in the oven
In a healthy veggie bake
But my favourite way of eating them
Is in a carrot cake

Ziki Buswell • Year 2
Broham Lower School
Bedfordshire

Toby Anstis
Radio DJ

The Cavalry is Coming

If you have a touch of flu
You know what you must do!
Slice up and orange or two
Add a lemon to the pan
Add water and honey
when you can!

Let it simmer until it's on the boil
It's really not too much toil
Drink it whilst it's hot
It will help you quite a lot
To conquer your flu like feelings
Oranges and Lemons with their peelings
Are vitamins indeed
Of that we are agreed!

Please use this remedy it's natural, it's real
And you will be fine
Well in no time!
It's a magical drink
With power so strong,

You can't go wrong!
Just make one every night
Until you feel just right

It's the orange that
Has the force
To make you well, of course!

It tastes delicious
But can be vicious
Whilst on the attack
Combating the flu
This is the recipe for me and you!
No matter what else you decide to do.

Cherries

Look what I have found
Cherries all red and round
Put them on your food
And you'll be in the mood
So eat cherries everyday
And shout HOORAY!
Put them on your ice cream
Yum! Yum! Yum!
Put them on your ice cream
And have some fun
At school open your packed lunch
Find the cherries and Munch! Munch! Munch!

Shauna Murphy • Year 2
Carleith Primary School
Scotland

Fruit and Veg and Me

There are many coloured vegetables
They are all good for you
Carrots are orange, I will eat a few
Beans are green, I will eat them too

My favourite fruit is apples
I like both green and red
They keep me nice and healthy
And out of my sick bed

Melons are sweet and juicy
Full of vitamin C
They quench my thirst on summer days
And help me climb trees

Hollie Connor • Year 2
Carr Primary School
Ireland

Fruit and Veg are Fun

Fruit and veg are fun to eat
As a snack or as a treat
Full of vitamins galore
That our body needs to store
Soft and sweet and crunchy too
What you eat is up to you
We all need five a day
To help us keep the colds away
Reds and greens and yellow and blue
Lots of colours to tempt you
Crunchy, munchy as you play
Ask your mum for some today

Sian Collis • Year 2
St James Primary School
Walsall

Cat Deeley

Television Presenter

The Orange Peeled By A Loved One's Hand

A humble orange taken from the bowl,
Peeled by my hand and eaten whole,
Tastes of sunshine and is so darn sweet,
It's a vitamin C-packed tasty treat.

But here's my question,
If I can be so bold,
Please be blunt,
The truth must be told,

The orange peeled with love,
By my friend,
Is a taste sensation,
I never want to end?

For an orange peeled by another's hand,
Has something special I don't understand,
A citrus explosion of indefinable greatness,
Of truly indescribable incomparable tastiness,

I could be wrong, I may not be correct.
But I'm gonna just say it ... Hedge all my bets!
A humble orange given and peeled with love,
Is a little slice of heaven, sent from above.

Fruit and Veg

Fruit and veg of every kind,
In every market you will find,
Apples and oranges are healthy to eat
Sweet and juicy – what a treat!

What type of veg would you like today?
Peas or carrots, you just say.

Rhubarb with custard,
Strawberries with cream,
Pineapple smoothie, oh what a dream,
Some of the best things in life are free,
Like picking apples from a tree.

Fruit and veg is good for me,
So I hope I have some for my tea.

Ryan Wheeler • Year 2
Eaton Primary School
Cheshire

Harvest Time

Harvest is a lovely time
Sometimes grey, sometimes blue
All harvest weathers are good for you

Fruit and nuts
Corn and veg
Lovely things grow on the hedge

And now it's time
To take them in
To cut cook and eat

So phone some friends
And let's meet

Amy Maloney • Year 2
Rawdon Littlemoor School
Leeds

Lisa Appignanesi
Award-winning Author

Apples

They gleam in the bowl
Round and succulent
Hang heavy in the branches
Eden before the fall
And as tempting.
Matisse paints them,
Green, golden, red
A bright mass of colour
To crunch and bite into
Sound, taste, sight, sense
All in one
Perfect
Apple

I am a Melon

I am a melon,
So juicy and sweet,
I dribble down your chin,
You can have me as a treat,
I am as round as a basketball
When you have finished,
Throw my skin in the dustbin.

Mia Cummings • Year 2
St Peter's CE Primary School
Bury

Jolyon Baker

Actor

The Spell of the Jersey Royals

There is a farm on Route de Vinchelez – the Alchemist's lair –
where you have to stoop and knock to enter the potato store
A dusty single electric bulb hangs by cobwebs
The earth-floored, granite-walled wooden lofted potato store.

Sometime in March – the Breton lady a White Witch –
hands to you in a brown paper bag the first Jersey Royals.
Grown with vraic from the sea on a steep cotil hand-dug,
hand-packed they glow with the promise of sunshine and
Winter's passing.

Rub off the sandy soil like Aladdin and his lamp add a
sprig of common mint – breathe in and boil.
First Jersey Royals – always make a wish
First Taste – Forgotten Taste – A wish come true.

I Love Vegetables and Fruit

Apples are sweet
Carrots are crunchy
Bananas are munchy
Oranges are scrummy
Pomegranates are yummy

Rebecca Evans • Year 2
The Abbey Junior School
Reading

Melon

Skin like a spider's web made of super glue
Honeycomb looking
Tropical island smelling
Makes me think of graceful, cabbage butterflies

Refreshing treat to have
Calming down treat to have
Inside seeds look like cornfields
Chewy and mouthwatering

Rippling like a river
Hard but moist inside

Shaumya Kularajan • Year 2
Moira House School
Eastbourne

Poem about Fruit

Apples and bananas,
They all grow on trees,
Oranges and cherries,
Oh, yes please!

Potatoes and carrots
Are all very yummy,
Cauliflower and peas,
Are lovely in my tummy.

Emily Curle • Year 2
Bruton Primary School
Somerset

Pomegranate

Purpley red in little bits
Oh how lumpy it is
My fingers get all sticky
Eat it with a cocktail stick
Get a knife and cut it in half
Red like cherries and apples
A very sweet fruit
Never eat the skin
A yummy scrummy fruit
To fill your tummy up
Eat it when it's raw it's …

Pomegranate!

Alicia Wood • Year 2
Our Lady's Convent School
Loughborough

Richard Hughes
Jockey

Marmalade

Best by far is marmalade
chunky cut with whisky
but I can manage Golden Shred
if the toast is crunchy.

Keep your strawberry conserves
in little plastic parcels.
I do not like such confitures
as found in second rate hotels.

Give me on my breakfast table
marmalade, the genuine,
dense with orange from Seville –
a rich and slightly bitter tang.

Best of all is marmalade
(it sees me through each day)
from the princely orange made
with skill and empathy.

Pumpkins

Oh perfect pumpkin
Only ever seen
Glowing as a lantern
Around Halloween

Oh perfect pumpkin
I love your orange skin
I think your colour is a delight
So I will eat you every night!

Charlie Peplow • Year 2
St Mary's Magdalen's Catholic School
London

The Colour of Health

Red is for pepper

Orange is for orange

Yellow is for lemon

Green is for apple

Blue is for blueberry

Purple is for cabbage

Violet is for aubergine

A colour a day keeps the doctor away

Sophie Cohn • Year 2
Manor Lodge School
Hertfordshire

Jamie Theakston
Radio DJ

Pie in the Sky

There's a knickerbocker glory
There's a flambé in the pan
There's a crush in the mixer

Just waiting for the bran
There's one sitting in the fruit bowl
About to get the chop
This is the definitely the fruit
That is Top of the Pops
There's a fool in the saucer
There's a float in the dish
There's a crumble in the oven
There's a banana covered fish
There's a whip that is swirling
There's a soufflé rising high
They've all gone bananas
There's a pie in the sky!

Harriet Scott

Radio DJ

Shallot

Shallot the onion was in a stew!

Was she Spanish or French,

She hadn't a clue?

She was cut up,

In pieces

She cried a lot

She just wanted to be

In a pickle pot!

Shallot Pickle

The Fruity Snowman Dream

I had a Christmas snowman dream
When I was lying in bed
Daddy came in and woke me up
'Hebe it's snowing!' he said

I cried with joy and happiness
Woke my brother up with a yawn
We both got dressed and ran downstairs
And ran out on the lawn

We made a white soft fruity snowman
As we snuggled in our clothes
Green grape eyes and rhubarb arms
And a banana for his nose

We gave him blueberry buttons too
And made him a snowman wife
Then I woke up and thought 'I'm only 7
And it's never snowed in my life'

So me and my brother went downstairs
Took some fruit and ice to bed
I squashed it with my reading book
And made a snowman smoothie instead

Hebe Foulsham • Year 2
Mells First School
Somerset

We are Fruit and Veg

I'm a tomato all red with pips
You can squash me and eat me with chips

I'm a potato round and heavy
Chip or mash me, then I'm ready

We are grapes, we grown on a vine
Squash me with you feet and I'll turn into wine

We are peppers, yellow, green or red
Eat me with salad or on a pizza

Chelsea Frost • Year 2
Bramford Primary School
Ipswich

What's in my Fridge

I eat a yellow banana,
And dance in my pyjamas

My mum gives me an apple to eat,
So I can stay on my feet

A cucumber is really really tall,
So I can eat it and swim deep in the pool!

My potato has no pips,
So my dad makes lovely chips!

The lemon is yellow like the sun,
And my family have lots of fun

Every morning my brain hops,
Because my tomato has a green star on the top!

Onions can be green, onions can be round,
But they always grow on the ground

Mum says 'eat your sprouts' and she always shouts,
I say yummy, yummy, they're in my tummy

Pomegranate pomegranate it's not for me,
I think I like my cup of tea!

Run, jump, play, football, karate, tennis too,
All these things I can do, because I eat my five a day,
That's my secret every day

Haran Arnar • Year 2
St John's Prep School
Potters Bar

Anthony Horowitz

Author

Tomatoes

When I hear politicians say
That we should eat five veg a day
I know at once what I must do –
I rush right out and join the queue
To purchase from my local store
Six tomatoes...maybe more
The ones I want (I know the type)
Are bright red, juicy, over-ripe
And then I find a good position
And throw them at the politician.

OVER-RIPE
TOMATOES

Apples

Apples apples in a line
Very soon they will be mine
Farmers are busy in the meadows
Cutting wheat and letting it dry
Up the hill and down the lane
Soon they will be home again

Tom Humphries • Year 3
Hunter Hall School
Cumbria

Does Fernando Torres
Eat Chillis?

Fernando Torres you are so fast
I wonder what gives you the blast
Do you eat a chilli before each match?
Are they from Spain in your own vegetable patch?
As you bite through the flesh, you'll hear the crunch
Your lips flare up, tingle and burn
You're sure to score a goal at every turn
Like a chilli pepper Fernando, you're so sizzling and spicy
I agree with you – chillis are sure nicey!

William James Pulle • Year 3
Holmes Chapel School
Cheshire

Annabel Karmel
Children's Food and Nutrition Writer

Picture Plate

A Floret forest

Of Broccoli trees

Cauliflower clouds

And scattered peas

In a pasta field

A vanilla pod gate

This imaginary story

Can be found on my plate!

Fruit and Vegetables Go ...

Peas go pop!

Apples go crunch

Bananas go squish

Carrots go crack

Potatoes go squash

Kiwis go scrape

Lemons go squeeze

Melons go poke

You go chomp chomp chomp

Tasty fruit and vegetables

Molly Dillingham • Year 3
William Shrewsbury Primary School
Staffordshire

Fruit and Vegetables

Fruit and vegetables are great
As long as they don't go out of date
Fruit can be sour or sweet
And like vegetables, are healthy to eat.
Fruit can be red orange and green
And taste nice with cream.
Vegetables are mainly coloured green
Just like the runner bean
They can both be juicy or dry
So why don't you giver them a try?

Kieran Patel • Year 3
St's Paul's School
Bolton

Anthea Turner

Television Presenter

Awesome Apple

I love apples and they love me
The reason I know is that they grow on my tree
I love to put them in my crumble
They make my tummy rumble
Thank you little apple for growing on my tree.

Fruit

The strawberries ripe and red
They remind me of blooming roses
Apples are crunchy and juicy
They remind me of leaves on a woodland floor
Carrots are orange and bright
They remind me of the evening sun
Setting before bedtime

Florence Barker • Year 3
Pulford Lower School
Bedfordshire

Fruits and Vegetables are go go go!

Curly cauliflowers
Pure and lumpy
Bright broccoli
Green and bumpy

Crunchy carrot sticks
Tall and thin
Sugary sweetcorn
Fresh not from a tin

Sweet strawberries
Luscious and squishy
A moon of melon
Juicy and slippery

Pearly peas
Round and small
Tangy tomatoes
Tucked into a ball

Bendy bananas
Sunny and proud
Polished potatoes
Fresh from the ground

All shapes, all sizes, all colours, all tastes
From all places, all countries
Fresh on our plates

Full of vitamins to help us grow
Fruits and vegetables are go go go!

Emma Shuker • Year 3
Eaton Primary School
Cheshire

I Like Aipples

I like aipples
Because aipples are sappie
Muckle and reid
Green and crisp
Aipples have a stalk

Nell MacDonagh • Year 3
Westruther Primary School
Scotland

Graham Taylor

Football Manager and Former Player

An Apple for Your Sweetheart

Granny can I have an apple
I asked with a twinkle in my eye
Of course you can she replied
As she put it in the pie.

Not in the pie I cried!
I want it fresh and sweet
To give to my sweetheart
When at the garden gate we meet.

You don't give an apple to your sweetheart
That really is a myth
And I should know of course
Because my name is Granny Smith.

I Wish

I wish I were an apple
Red juicy and round
When I'm ripe and ready
I'll fall to the ground

I wish I were a carrot
Orange long and bright
I'd help all the children
See in the night

I wish I were a banana
Yellow and shaped like the moon
All mushy and soft on the end of my spoon

I wish I were a pea
Small, round and good for you
I'd go on your roast dinner
With cauliflower too

Lauren Aherne • Year 3
Pope Paul Catholic School
Hertfordshire

If Fruit Could Talk

"Psst, hey you…..here, yes over here
We all live together, we're the Earth's friends forever

To some we are yucky
And they don't think they're lucky
To bite into our skin
And drink juices within

Some people like chocolate, sweeties and pies
But who could not love our shape and our size?

We're green. Purple, black, orange, and red
We give lots of vitamins and strength it is said

The magic number is 5 to eat everyday
To help keep the colds and sore tummies away

We're good for your diet, we keep babies quiet
So please don't forget us and give us a thought
Next time you are peckish
Hide those biscuits you bought!

Psst! Hey you….we won't disappoint you
Our word we do give
We're the family of fruit
Over here, in the bowl…..where we live!

Savannah Ives • Year 3
St Joseph & St Teresa's Catholic Primary School
Doncaster

Bill Paterson

Actor

Let's call the whole thing what

How does the song go?
Ah, yes.

'You say Tomatoes
And
I say Tomatoes'

'You say Potatoes
And
I say Potatoes'

'Potatoes, potatoes'

'Tomatoes, tomatoes'

Sorry to interrupt.
But
Wouldn't it be easier
if we both just said
Vegetables?

Well, no.
Because botanically
the Tomato is a
Fruit.

I see.

Clever chap
that Gershwin.

Quince

In our garden we have a quince tree
Bees come to the blossom
In September we pick the fruit
Golden and furry and plump
Raw they are hard and sour –
But when mummy cooks them in sugar and wine
They are my favourite fruit ever

Freya Kay • Year 3
Manor Lodge School
Hertfordshire

The Mango Tango

I am a mango and I do the tango
I eat mango while I do the tango
I am a tango mango!
Get it?
I am a mango tango

Amie Smithers • Year 3
St Johns CE Primary School
Essex

Piers Morgan

TV Presenter and Journalist; Former Editor of the

Daily Mirror

Banana's Split with Pea

It's good news week,
Banana's **_split_** with pea
They were the most unlikely **_pear_**
I think you will agree!

Banana's just a **_crumble_**
And his feelings are quite dashed
He's so browned off, this speckled chap
He simply feels quite **_mashed!_**

Banana feels that he's a *float*
And feels just like a *fool*
He's *whipped* into a frenzy
Because he broke the rule!

The mix together of fruit and veg
Is difficult you see!
But both of them are great alone
Tasted individually!

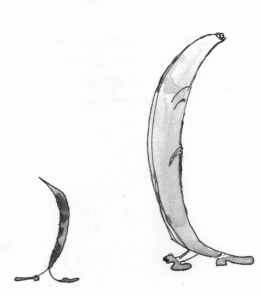

The Pumpkin

Oh pumpkin, oh pumpkin, you wondrous thing

With your beautiful shiny orange skin

You start as a seed planted in spring

All summer long listening to birds sing

You grow and grow

Until before there is snow

Now autumn is here

And it's the time of the year

When your job is to fill us with fear

We cut out your mouth nose and eyes

To give all our friends a scary surprise

As day turns to night

You face comes alight

It's trick or treat

So give me something sweet

Oh pumpkin oh pumpkin

It's Halloween!

Mollie Emms • Year 3
Lympne Primary School
Kent

The Vegetable Stall

On my way to school
I walk past a vegetable stall
I hear people speaking to the owner Bill
And saying
'Can I have this?'
'Can I have that?'
I also hear the owner shouting at the customers
He shouts 'buy one get one free!'

I see the beautiful colours of the vegetables
Green bright broccoli
The orangey orange carrots
The ripe red tomatoes
It makes me want to buy a delicious red pepper
Which goes juicy and crunchy in my mouth

Tahlia Klein • Year 3
Cavendish Primary School
Chiswick

Jon Sayers
Poet

The Boot of Fruit – A Tale of Fruity Insurrection

There was an old woman, who lived in a boot.

She fed all her children on fruit, fruit – and fruit.

They had berries for breakfast, lemons for lunch,

At tea-time a tray of tomatoes to munch.

And at supper – the biggest fruit-fest of all –

The table resembled a greengrocer's stall:

Oranges, melons, grapes, nectarines,

Apricots, peaches, plums, tangerines

Rolled around in a glorious pageant of colour.

But those kids couldn't think of anything duller!

One Sunday they felt that they'd just had enough

Of the tree-hanging, ground-growing, juice-bursting stuff.

'Yuck!' they declared, spitting out pips,

And wiping the juices clean from their lips.

'Ick!' they exclaimed, chucking fruit skin

With violence into the kitchen swing bin.

'Ugh!' they cried out, crushing the peel

With a fist or an elbow, a knee or a heel.

Their old mother's mouth hung agape and aghast.

She knew that she had to say something fast.
'PACK IT IN!' she yelled, sensing the start of a riot.
'Pray what is the cause of your flamin' disquiet?'
'Fruit' piped the eldest, with the courage and pride
Of knowing you have Right and Truth on your side,
'Should form only part of a well-balanced diet!'
Then he added, his young eyes flashing with zeal,
'In ITSELF, it does NOT make a NUTRITIOUS MEAL!'

Well, his brothers and sisters, they clapped and
they cheered
And the old woman stared at the brood she had reared.
'And how shall we balance your diet, I pray?'
'With five other foodstuffs, at least, every day.
We want fish, we want meat, we want bread, eggs,
and rice,
And sometimes some vegetables, too, would be nice.
And if we don't get them, we're all Leaving Boot,
'cause we're sick of the fruit and the fruit. And the fruit.'
Was the old woman stunned? Was the old woman cross?
Did she feel that you have to show children who's boss?
Was the old woman hurt? Was the old woman stung?
Or did she believe you can learn from the young?
Well, if on a walk or a bike ride one day,
You happen to stray along Fruity Boot Way,
You'll see for yourself the end to this fable:

In one boot you'll spy a large, happy table.
Yes, through the boot's eyelets, behind the boot's laces
You'll glimpse the bright smiles of well-nourished faces,
A great wealth of foods gracing each plate and cup
And a woman so proud of the kids she's brought up.

Tomato

I am a tomato
Very very nice
I taste even better
When I'm very ripe

We make it into ketchup
We make it into sauce
We put it on a salad
And on pizza of course

Benedict Williams • Year 3
The Elms Primary School
Nottingham

Watermelon!

Red green,
Shiny and clean,
Round and smooth
Is the way it should be
And what's inside waiting for me?

Deep red deliciously ripe,
Hiding pips as black as night
I close my eyes and take my first bite
I never forget the taste, even at night,

It's so refreshing on a hot summer day
Especially when you come in from play.

Saskia Collins • Year 3
Ann Edward School
Gloucestershire

Gladstone Small
Former England Cricketer

A Bowl of Sunshine

If you want a **bowl** of sunshine
Barbados is the place
By the turquoise Caribbean
Just enjoy it's style and grace

If you want to have a **paddle**
The sea is seldom rough
You can **hit the deck**, just relax
This is certainly the stuff

It's where **maidens** munch on Mangoes
This fruit is just the thing
So sweet and so delicious
They make the monkeys **swing**

The locals are so friendly
They love to stop and chat
And sometimes just at twilight
You may just spot a **bat**

Mango punch with a touch of rum
Can lure you down the *track*
The taste of fruit from Barbados
Will help you ***bend your back!!***

Enjoy enjoy,
Run, jump and hop
Enjoy Barbados fruit
It's a ***lollipop***

What Would I Be?

Fruit or veg what would I be?
A crunchy carrot or celery
A bright orange pumpkin with a scary face
A fresh frilly lettuce that looks like lace

A rosy red apple, juicy and sweet
A pretty red raspberry such a treat

If I was an onion
I might make you cry
A chopped potato
You might like to fry

I quite like the look of peas in their pods
Their colour reminds me of sweet little frogs

Or I could be a bean all dangly and green
But I really don't mind
And it would be unkind
To say I prefer one from the other

Stephanie Adamson • Year 3
The Abbey Junior School
Reading

94

Broccoli

I'm as green as a slippery, slimy frog

Chew me with a marvellous delectable roast dinner

I look like a tall towering tree but I am tinier

My first letter is in bike but not in like

My last letter is in sit but not in sat

What am I?

Rachel Meehan • Year 4
R L Hughes Primary School
Wigan

Hannah Sandling

Stylist and Television Presenter

Fruity Friendship

It's such a good job that apples and pears are the best
of friends
With strawberries, kiwis and with grapes my happiness
does depend.
In one big bowl, together they hang,
I can't think of a better treat
Best buddies, sitting side by side,
Fruit salad is just neat

Eat Your Veggies

I'm a vegetarian
I don't eat meat
Vegetables to me
Are a tasty treat

Celery so crunchy
Carrots so munchy
Who needs steak
When you've got 'Broccoli Bake'?

Vegetables are healthy
And give you energy
There are lots of varieties
Try one and you'll see

So when you're in a shop
Grab some veggies not a chop
Don't put meat upon your plates
And the animals will be your mates

Abbie Cox • Year 4
The Abbey Junior School
Reading

Food For Thought

Oranges give vitamin C
Apples give you energy
Grapes can make a yummy treat
Even though they are not a sweet

Chips and mushy peas are fine
Just don't eat them all the time
If you do you might get ill
Not to mention the chip shop bill!

A balanced diet is all you need
So think of this next time you feed
Too many sweets are bad for your teeth
And later in life will cause you grief

So what this poem is trying to say
Eat fruit and veg … at least five a day!
But don't forget occasionally
You can have chips and sausages for your tea!

Thomas Hibbs • Year 4
Holmes Chapel Primary School
Cheshire

Jilly Johnson
Model

The 613 Pomegranate

The Pomegranate is a curious fruit,
That doesn't choose to follow suit.

Slice it open and spotted inside,
Six hundred and thirteen seeds trying to hide.

Encompassed in glowing pink juice,
They dislodge easily, becoming loose.

These dark seeds have a mystical meaning,
Which is why they are worth gleaning.

Representing good deeds that men should do,
Don't believe it, then count a few too.

Fruit Can ...

Apples and pears can run up the stairs
Oranges and lemons chase the melons
Pomegranates and peaches search the beaches
Berries and cherries ride on ferries

Carrots help you to see in the dark
Potatoes and tomatoes like to take part
Brussels and beans make you mean
And lastly broad beans make you green

Grace Goodrich • Year 4
St John's CE Primary School
Essex

Healthy Eating

Healthy eating is the best
Eat some today, save the rest
And if you really want a snack
Later go and get a pack
Take some now, it's really good
How could I now as big as a hood
You really know your healthy stuff so come round
and get as much

Eating healthy's really great
And eat it early, eat it late
Tingle tingle goes the bell
Illnesses illnesses, it kills them well
Now we're nearly done
Go and get some it's really fun

Arielle Nahari • Year 4
Bury and Whitefield Jewish Primary School
Bury

Dermot O'Leary

Television Presenter

Veg

I love my British Fruit and Veg,
But I need it when it's ripe and fresh,
To get my one of five, flown in by air
To me, seems an awful mess.

We've got so much to eat and drink,
There doesn't seem a reason,
To send fresh produce around the world,
When we can eat in season.
In Springtime I love my roots and greens,
Like Carrots, Leeks and Sorrell,
In Summertime I love red berries so,
I'm sure it's hard to quarrel.

Asparagus, and Jersey Royals,
Complete my summer fare,
Just as the leaves to turn a golden brown,
And there comes a chill in the air.

Autumn means a loved return,
Of Apples, Corn and Plums,

To crunch or stew, crumble or bake,
So long as they're in my tum.

And then the still of winter comes,
So we need a hearty table,
Of Turnips, Suede and Cabbage,
And that completes my fable.

So to conclude go out today,
And support your local Greengrocer,
Because food tastes great wherever it's from,
But better when it's closer.

LOCALLY GROWN

Ingans

When ma mammie chaps ingans
It maks ma een water
Ingans hae lots o'skiffles
Maybe roughly fifty
Ingans guff very strang
They're just a bit soor
When I eat thaim
They mak ma tounge tingle

Katie Marwick • Year 4
Westruther Primary School
Scotland

Sinitta

Singer and Presenter

The Pineapple

The pineapple isn't a pine,
The tree that produces the cones.

The pineapple isn't an apple,
The fruit that has pips not stones.

The pineapple is an ananas,
Yellow, chunky and sweet.

Making Pina Colada into a real tropical treat.

If You Don't Eat Your Vegetables!

My mum always goes blabbing on about what I won't be
able to do if I don't eat my vegetables.
Here are some of the things she says …

If you don't eat your carrots, then you won't be able to see
in the dark
If you don't eat your spinach, then you won't be able to
help the deliverymen move the furniture when you're older

I don't believe any of the things she said about vegetables
I thought maybe one day she'd say……

If you don't eat your peas, then you won't turn green and
be able to talk to the aliens

If you don't eat your sprouts then you won't grow tall
enough to fight the giants

If you don't eat your sweetcorn, then you won't be able to
slay a dragon

But one day I *did* eat all my vegetables and guess what?
did turn green and I *could* talk to the aliens!

And I ***did*** grow tall enough to fight the giants and I managed to slay a dragon that same day

So from now on, to my mum's surprise, I always eat my vegetables … well, all except for my cabbage!

Ella Drury • Year 4
Westdale Junior School
Nottinghamshire

Joanne Harris

Author

The Battle of the Fruit and Veg

General Grape and Private Pea
Went rolling into battle
With Captain Carrot, Sergeant Spud
And Sub-Lieutenant Apple.

The enemy was long and sharp.
His name was Evil Reg.
He led a band of kitchen knives
Against the fruit and veg.

They fought all day, they fought all night
With awesome bravery
And many of the soldiers fell
Both sweet and savoury.

Olga Okra, Percy Peach
And Albert Avocado
All died, alongside Chris Courgette
And Timothy Tomato.

Still, there is a silver lining to
This melancholy ballad.
I put them all into a soup
And a nice fruit salad.

No More Bananas!

I know they give you energy
But they're just not for me
'Please no bananas for my tea!'
I know they have vitamins
But they're just not for me
'Please no bananas for my tea!'
Unless of course they are in a smoothie
Then I'd have three for my tea

Yummy!

Elliot Wall • Year 4
The Butts Primary School
Hampshire

Rumble in the Fruit Bowl

Who is inside the fruit bowl?
Oh look deep inside

There is Mr Braeburn, Mrs Cox,
Granny Smith knitting socks,

There's Sir Williams with Lady Pink
Masta Jaffa with his funny wink

There's Señora Valencia, Monsieur Gala
All sitting in the fruit bowl parlour

Ellie Ladopouli • Year 4
Hadley Wood School
London

The Big Quarrel

One marker day on the vegetable stall
The vegetables argued
Who's the best of them all

Red headed carrots
Hair in bunches
'We're the prettiest and the crunchiest'

Then leek stood up
White and tall
'I'm the most handsome on the stall'

French beans exclaimed
'We're the most trendy
Have a lovely figure
Slim and bendy'

Green leafy cabbage said
'I've had enough
Going to tell you the truth
It might be quite tough

Health before beauty
Nutrition not looks
That's what you're here for
Before you get cooked!

Antonia Hilton • Year 4
Pope Paul Catholic Primary School
Hertfordshire

The Last Day of the Apple

I am sitting in the fruit bowl
Waiting to be eaten

This is my last day
In the warm bowl
Snuggled up with the banana

I've a fiery stalk
To remind me
Of my happy days on the tree in Autumn

I've a dead bit
At my bottom
To remind me when I was full of glee
As blossom on the tree

Iona Kininmonth • Year 4
Godolphin Prep
Wiltshire

Michaela Morgan

Children's Author and Poet

High Five!

Clementines
Tangerines
Nectarines too.
If you like fruit
Just shout Who Hoo!

Bananas in custard
Apples in a pie
If you like fruit
Make a High Five!

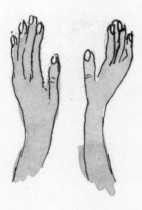

The Midnight Fight

Broccoli boasted, 'Veggies are the best'
Peach cried, 'Fruits, let's put it to the test'
Strawberry suggested, 'let's have a fight'
At exactly twelve o'clock midnight!

The battle was raging
Stampeding, rampaging
Spinach turned slushy
Mango became mushy

Courgette kicked melon off the stool
While cucumber stayed perfectly cool
'Squish' went orange (vitamin C)
'Slap' went banana (vitamin D)

Until a hungry human came in
With a napkin tucked under his chin
Slice, slice, slice
Dice, dice, dice

Then the human began to eat
His very nutritious treat
Munch, munch, munch
Crunch, crunch, crunch

Mmmmmmmm!

Vikram Ramaswamy • Year 4
University College School
London

The Ugly Fruit

All alone and sad
I am feeling so bad
I'm all lumpy, not cute
And I'm called ugly fruit

The other fruits tease
They can be really mean
They think they're great
The best to be seen

I'm all yellow and tall
When you're just so small
Boast banana
Up high in his tree

The grape laughs out loud
He's really so proud
It's such a shame
But it's all in your name
I'm small and I'm sweet
I grow on a vine
I can even make wine!

Apple sniggers at ugly fruit
As smug as can be
'You're just one colour
I'm many of these
And I survey the world
From up in my tree'

The ugly fruit sighs
'So I might not be cute
I'm just who I am
I'm just ugly fruit
But we all know our fate
To end up on a plate
No matter how handsome we are.'

Cathal Gilmour • Year 4
St Mary Magdalen's Catholic School
London

Julie Christie

Actress

Oh Brussel Sprout

Oh Brussel sprout
So small and stout
I feel so glad
That you're about

But now, alas
No time for talk
I'm going to spear you
With my fork,
Spear you
With my fork.

Yummy Carrots

I was a little seed
They put me in the ground
They covered me with soil
I was nowhere to be found.

Sun and rain beat down on me
I slowly began to grow
I knew I had to hurry up
Before the first white snow.

Up through the soil
I poked my bright green head
My carrots are nearly ready
The cheeky farmer said.

My body is turning bright orange
A couple more weeks to go
And then the cheeky farmer
In his tractor he will sow.

Harvest time is here now
To the shops I'm on my way
Nice and clearly packaged
For you to eat one day.

Nikola Kepska • Year 4
Thorpe Hesley Junior School
Rotherham

Christopher Biggins

Actor and winner of *I'm a Celebrity ...*

Get Me Out Of Here!

King of the jungle

As King of the jungle

You have to be cute
If your favourite dessert
Is half a grapefruit

To trudge through the camp
Full of insects and slime
To look for a grapefruit
And then find a lime!

To search through the bush
For this breakfast treat
An orange won't do
So just grit your teeth

Don't be a lemon
Keep searching until
A grapefruit is found
Just have a strong will

Half a grapefruit's a must
For a king or a fool
In the jungle of life
It's just a jewel!

Vegetable Hat

If I could choose a vegetable
To wear upon my head
A tomato would be my first choice
Nice and juicy red

Around the sides and up the back
A few carrots I would stick
Then I'd add some broccoli
From the garden I would pick

Afterwards I'd put them all
Into a great big bowl
And make them all into a soup
With a crusty garlic roll

William Sharman • Year 4
Peterborough High School
Peterborough

A Fruity Poem

Oranges, bananas, peaches and grapes,
Different colours, tastes and shapes.
Fruit is so juicy and tasty too,
I like red berries mixed with blue.
A really ripe pear, some strawberries and cream
It makes my mouth water when I dream,
Of a super fruit salad served up in a dish,
After my dinner of sensible fish.
Fruit is full of vitamins we're told,
I'll look like a banana when I grow old.
I eat one each day for potassium you see
Much better than chocolate and cakes for tea!

Mercedes Main • Year 5
Cestria School
Co Durham

A Rumba for a Cucumber

I like the short ones
The flavour is more distinct
But when you have a long one
It's like eating a drink

Dark green on the outside
Light green within
Yummy in sandwiches
Pickled in a tin
Sliced in a salad
Dipped into humus
A sushi roll without it is
Never a bonus

Some like them peeled
I prefer the skin
I cry when they wrinkle
And I have to put them in the bin

When I'm in bed and in a slumber
My dreaming wish is of Cucumber

Gil Shani • Year 5
University College School
London
133

Marina Fiorato

Children's Author

Ode to a Courgette

If you were to hear the word 'Courgette'
You may well remark; 'I'll bet
That vegetable is French.'
And you might
Just be right.
We Italians say Zucchini;
An exotic name for something ... greeny.
Courgette or Zucchini?
The question's unsolvable
Like Istanbul
Versus Constantinople.
But this I'll say to end my theme:

That if you seek the long and green
Amongst the vegetable scene
Then don't forget
The British Courgette
Nor shun the
Cucumber.

Lisa Butcher

Model and Television Presenter

The Queen the Mangosteen

The Mangosteen is a tropical evergreen
It is sweet and tangy with the flavour of peach
It is really not so accessible and quite out of reach
If you're a local in China you can enjoy the treat
Of finding a Mangosteen to eat.

This regal fruit originated from the land of Asia
The kingdom of Thai, Cambodia and Annam
If you visit the markets in Chinatown in Europe and the US
You may be able to find the Mangosteen today!

I expect you will now start your trail
Don't give up, you must not fail!

Apple Tree

I'm lonely against the raging wind,
No leaves on my bare bones,

Warmth thawing,
I'm growing again,
I flick out my buds to the cool open air.

My petals can see the sun.
I can feel the spring breeze.

Infinitesimally small beginnings
Evolving into apples that you can gourmandize,
Savour the tantalizing taste of fruity lusciousness,
Mouth wateringly scrumptious.

Leon Bozianu • Year 5
Newport Primary School
Essex

Rita Simons

Actress – aka Roxy in *EastEnders*

What am I?

I'm thick skinned, hard, and quite green

Do you know what I mean?

When ripe

I'm known to blush

I'm cool,

But easy to crush

I'm soft in the middle

But by the end of this riddle

You'll know what I am!

I sometimes feel seedy

But even if you are greedy

You'd be full

If you consumed all of me

Although I am round

In Japan I can be found to be different,

I'm even square

I'm not always red

But let it be said

I normally am

And can be made into jam!

But the best place to take me

Is off to the beach

For a picnic,

No I'm not a peach!

I'm a Melon,

Yes I'll keep you trim

I'm a lover of water

So enjoy a swim

When you visit the sea

In the Rays of the Sun

Don't go alone, take me!

As I'm the one

To keep you refreshed

I'm so good to eat

It will make your visit

A special treat!

Dates Dates Dates

Dates have the smell of gingery raisins,
The taste of toffees mixed with honey,
They feel so sticky and squishy like mashed potatoes,
It looks as wrinkly as the trunk of a dark, dull tree.

Waqar Hussain • Year 5
Kingsway Primary School
Warwickshire

Down in the Orchard, What Do I See?

Some are as ripe as the sun coming out,
Like the sun's sunset.

It feels like a ball as bumpy as an old mans wrinkles.
I feel the juice dripping down my hands.

When you drink it, it has a sweet flavour, as sweet
as sugar.
ere are so many flavours, like your taste buds are having
a party!

I smell the citrus

What is it?

An orange!

Shivani Bhatt • Year 5
All Saints C of E Primary School
Wimbledon

143

Nick Lander
Restaurant Critic

Asparagus Spears

Our battle only lasts a season
The few short summer months
Our slim army advances and retreats
Between avocados, peas and leeks.

No steely blades our weapons sound
No lethal bullets do we send
Instead our spears just gently bend,
Lean softly towards the ground.

There are some who hold it more profane
To remain lined up tight in cellophane
Than to advance in military formation
Towards inevitable blood and devastation.

Yet ours is a sorrowful fight:
The relentless lot of deep green spears
A conflict never lost and never won
Just repeated through the years

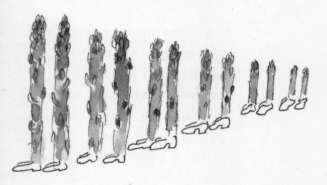

Lester 'Zoom' Headley
Author

The Caribbean Banana

I am often curved
I can make you strong
I am firm
I am yellow
I am a very friendly fellow.

I am sometimes green
But never mean
I am easily seen
I am one from a bunch
Bite into me now and take a crunch.

I have two skin tones
Green when I am growing
With the 'Ray of Sunshine' upon my body
I am now yellow, take some of me, and have your say
For I can put a smile upon your pretty face

146

Farmer and planters alike, they love to see me
And so you should love to partake with ease
Just reach out your hand, take me and see
Smile before you bite into me
Rub your tummy, and smile if you please

I am the triple sweet yellow Caribbean banana!

Fruit and Vegetables

I like apples, I like pears,
I like eating them upstairs,
Bananas, strawberries I like too,
Plenty there for me and you,
Potatoes, carrots and swede
Build my muscles and help me read
Broccoli, cabbage and runner beans
Help me grow to be a teen

Owain John • Year 5
Llansteffan Primary School
Wales

Gillian Slovo

Author

The Mango Tango

Mango learned to tango several years ago,
Starring in the exotic Tropical Fruit Salad Show.
Lychee, Papaya and Melon taught the steps,
Mango reckoned this was as good as it gets.

Huge audiences watched the spectacular,
Rave reviews given in the vernacular.
Mango and Kiwi were the renowned duo,
But sadly nothing lasts forever – hey ho.

Seeing the potential for something more spartan,
An industrialist squeezed them both into a carton.
Someday they will be back on their feet
Wowing the crowds with the Latin beat.

Fruit Salad Bowl

I will put in my bowl

The soft squishy feel of the crescent moon banana,
The zingy smell of a saffron lemon,
The extraordinary taste of the yellow, fruity sun.

I will put it in my bowl

The sweet unusual flavour of crimson strawberries,
With their bumpy texture from the enchanted exterior,
And the blissful bounce of their cheerful crop.

I will put it in my bowl

The rough touch of a fizzing kiwi,
The peculiar taste of a gleaming green pear
And the exotic smell of the hot pink pomegranate.

My bowl is fashioned from pineapple skin,
And shinning apple seeds as black as coal,
With tangerine pieces on the edges,
In the corners you'll find coconuts,
With milk as smooth as velvet.

Lucy Higgens • Year 5
R L Hughes Primary School
Wigan

151

David Gower

Former England Cricketer

I Wandered Lonely As A Grape

I wandered lonely as a grape
That drops off from the bunch
And rolls around the table top
Not destined now for lunch

Wobbling on t'ward the edge
Then falling like a log,
Landing splat, upon the floor
To be sniffed at by the dog.

Next kicked about by sightless
Feet 'til just a soggy mess.
Then at last swept away
To no-one's great distress.

This story's moral is
A grape's a fruit but not
A grapefruit. Poets, this
must never be forgot!

A grape's no use on its own.
It's doomed if cut loose.
Need a fruity simile?
Choose a pamplemousse.

Fruits of Nature

I would like the world to be a better place,
I would like everyone to have a smiling face.
All the children to eat fruit and veg
And all the peas to bounce over the hedge!

The grapes will hop in the sunshine,
The kiwis will sing in the sky!
Music will flow and poems will rhyme and
onions will fly very high!

The pears will play on cellos,
The lychees will fry marshmallows.
The corn will play hid and seek in the hay!
And the apples will keep the doctors away!

And what about the bluest of blueberries?
Who will have the latest of blackberries?
The oranges will tango with lemons and lime!
Lets hope the melons will have a great time!!

The world will be happy and jolly,
The children will not reach for a lolly.
They will merrily eat fruit of nature
And be nice to all of the creatures.

Nicole Boran • Year 5
The James Oglethorpe Primary School
Essex

Oh Why Can't it be 10 a Day!

If it was 1 a day I would choose a peach.
Soft, pink and red.
Dribbling juice, sticking to my face.

If it was 2 a day I would choose a peach and an apple.
Shiny, red and green.
Crunching and crisp in my mouth.

If it was 3 a day I would choose a peach, an apple and
a banana.
Spotty, squishy and yellow.
Peeling back the skin with my fingertips.

If it were 4 a day I would choose a peach, an apple,
a banana and strawberries.
Plump, ripe and smelling sweet.
Picking from the garden on a warm summers day.

If it were 5 a day I would choose a peach, an apple,

a banana, strawberries and a pineapple.

Spiky, golden and brown.

Bringing alive my taste buds.

Oh how I would love it to be 10 a day!

Catherine Gray • Year 5
Eaton Primary School
Cheshire

Maureen Lipman

Actor, Author and Poet

Inevitable Call to the Vegetable Ball

Professor Papaya and Doctor Date,

Curers of primary Neuroses,

Are having a bash

to generate cash

For neurofibromatosis.

Nurse Cherry Tomato and Ma and Pa 'Snip,

Sell trinkets both modern and quaint,

And twelve pear shaped waiters

Gild swedes and potatoes

For dosh to erase this complaint.

A quartet of string beans play Gershwin,

Rhapsody in Blueb'ries in C,

While a Bach variation

Fills the crowd with elation

And a Damson duets with a Pea.

The auction and raffle are mammoth
Leeked Martha the Guava who ran it.
Egged on by a Radish
the total's so lavish
We'll kick this disease off the planet!

Tracey Haines

Writer

Five a Day

Succulent strawberries covered with seeds
crunchy carrots tempting a bite
lively lettuce carpets the plate
cherry tomatoes, round, red and ripe.

Bushy broccoli, a miniature forest
cauliflower sporting a white head of hair
stripey celery in regiment order
bulbous fennel, green and fair.

Prickly pineapple poised to prepare,
mouthwatering melon quenching the thirst
little green grapes paired up with purple
overflowing with vitamins, ready to burst.

Reg

There was an old gardener called Reg
Who had become an expert on veg.
Broccoli, carrots and peas,
Turnips, leeks and green beans
Were surrounded by Reg's high hedge.

The rabbits came without invitation,
And started to eat the vegetation.
Reg got distressed
His mind in a mess,
And soon was on serious medication!

India Wild • Year 5
Godolphin Prep
Wiltshire

Sweet Soft Strawberry

Oh beautiful strawberry
You're as soft as a pillow
As spotty as a spotty dog
You're as red as the devil's skin
However spotty you are I still like you
Even though I will eat you, you will still be in my dream

Oh beautiful strawberry
You're as sharp as a pin
You're squishy and squelshy
You're as delicate as a friend
You can be small like a little mouse
You can be big like a bouncing balloon
Even though I will eat you, you will still be in my dream.

Olivia Croggan • Year 5
Thorpe Hesley Junior School
Rotherham

Diane Samuels

Playwright

What am I?

There once was a tree in Iran
That bore the first fruit that I am
My arils are sweet
If I'm ripe when you eat
And if not they're as bitter as sin

So whose seeds could possibly be
Pure temptation for Persephone?
Tis I sealed her fate
Yes, a pomegranate
And I'm packed full of vitamin C!

Ten Juicy Apples

One smiling grandpa sits and eats a pear,
Two small babies munch grapes in a high chair,
Three cheeky brothers dine on strawberries sweet,
Four giggling sisters chew plums in the heat,
Five kind aunties swallow pineapples merrily,
Six ripe oranges picked by cousins carefully,
Seven naughty nephews grabbing cherries red and roun
Eight lovely nieces nibble melons, making lots of sound
Nine friendly uncles all eating a peach
Ten juicy apples, just out of my reach!

Eleanor Smith • Year 5
Robert Kett Junior School
Wymondham

Laurie Phillips
Author

Great God Beetroot (with apologies to Henry Wadsworth Longfellow)

Should you ask me whence this poem,
Whence these vegetables and fruits,
With the odours of the garden,
With the worms and caterpillars,
With the curling smoke of bonfires,
With the planting of small patches,
With the frequent sweat and digging,
And natural compost fertilising,
Growing from recycled waste.

I should answer, I should tell you:
From the green grass of my garden,
From the can and water barrel,
From the land on which my house stands, Close to
Christchurch, near to Bournemouth, From the seaside,
sands and waters, close to marshland, reeds and rushes,
Amongst the seagulls and the bird pooh.

I repeat this poem as I heard it,
From the lips of Great God Beetroot,
Legends of Carrots and Potatoes,
Turnips, Parsnips, and Tomatoes,
Radish, different kinds of Lettuce,
Cucumbers and Broad beans climbing,
In the garden, climbing, climbing,
In the veg patch growing, growing,
Overwhelmed by beauteous bounty.

God Beetroot told me not to tell you,
Great God Beetroot say it's secret,
In the Autumn, digging deeply,
In the Winter, in my wellies,
In the wet rain and the cold snow,
In the spring, begin the planting,
In beds so fertilised and fragrant,
In the summer, see the blossoms,
Collect the veg, fresh daily eating.

Great God Beetroot, he's the wise veg,
He knows best, makes children grow,
He says eat five fruits and veggies,
He says you must eat them daily,
He says it makes you fit and healthy,
He wants you to be fit and healthy,
You heed the words of Great God Beetroot, Knows
more than a school full of teachers, He should really
be Headmaster.

Sara Midda
Author

If

If the world's greatest poets
With seeds to sow, writ
Verses in praise –
Of potatoes and maize
Lettuces and leeks
All planted in rows,
Tomatoes and peas

Perhaps they did – or not
Perhaps they drank soup
Through a widened straw
Ate vegetables raw
Or in salads and stews, on pasta or rice,
Bean curd – so nice
All so delicious and even nutritious
They forgot about words
So carried away by freshest of veggies
And looked forward to fruit

Of similar repute and just danced round in glee
At the thought of a pea
Once a prized possession
Being valued again
By all women and men

The Berry Family

Once there was a blackberry
Who got married to a raspberry.

They had a boy called blueberry
And lived happily till spring.

Alas! They had a girl
She was round and looked like a pearl

Everyone was merry,
Until they realised she was a cherry.

They took her to Dr. Strawberry
His surgery was on a hill.

'There is nothing wrong with your daughter,
Just give her a sip of water.'

'But doctor she is a cherry,
We are a family of berries!'

He replied: 'There is no problem with that,
You are a family and that's that!'

Agnes Fanning • Year 5
The Abbey School
Reading

Esther Rantzen

Television Presenter

Turn Over A New Leaf!

A Spinach wilting on a shelf
Was whispering sadly to himself,
'I wish I had been born a bean
With scarlet blooms and tendrils green
Or sweet corn golden in the sun
Or orange carrots, they're such fun!
But no, I'm spinach, here I sit
Unloved, unwanted, I could spit,'
But while he moaned, with gloomy looks
Along came crowds of tv cooks,
Delia, Jamie, Gordon too
And all the 'Ready Steady' crew.
They leaped on Spinach with a shout,
'Now this is what we're all about!
Let's steam and chop him, mix with cream
Or bacon bits, now that's a dream!'
They grabbed a bunch, and then some more,
Inventing recipes galore
With salt and pepper, what a dish!
They added him to eggs and fish
And with the few sprigs they had left

Spinach came top in Masterchef!
So here's the moral. Don't despair
If no one seems to love or care,
You too can realise your dream
If you're prepared to join a team.
Spinach was once a dull green leaf
Who just got stuck in people's teeth,
But tossed in a salad, creamed in a pot,
Hurrah – he's cool, he's hot!

The Pomegranate

You have
Smooth, but scarred skin,
Hard and uninviting to eat,
Greasy, dark yellow and sharp points on top.

But then

I cut you in half,
Revealing your glittering jewels,
Bright scarlet translucence with little
Black seeds inside.
Just like the treasure in a Geode!

Lucy Toom-Smith • Year 5
Westdale Junior School
Nottinghamshire

Twiggy
Model

Life's Bowl of Cherries

We're on a platter
But it doesn't matter
Who should be mixing
With who!
A combination
Of dubious flirtation,
Banana and
Blackcurrant brew!
We can all chatter
And then we can scatter
To a bowl
That we never knew!
Then there's the clatter
Of spoon meeting dish
Of pear meeting apple
And then there's the wish
That we want to come true
Pure harmony
Of love and devotion
And true integration
Will become a fruit salad

Of mixed fruit and berries
For this tuneful ballad
Of Life's bowl of cherries

Tommy

I'm waiting. I'm waiting in the greenhouse
For you to admire my blushing pride.
'I Tommy T'
Here I am ripe and ready, please pick me,

Pillar-box red, fresh and juicy
My time is now, full of flavour
As a sauce or in a bottle I'm yours to savour

Think of me as one of your daily five
I'll look good with a lettuce at my side
Perhaps I can tempt you grilled or fried!

Feel my firm skin, think of my taste
I'm waiting, this is my time, this is my fate
Go on, I'm YOUR tomato – put me on your plate.

Maxim Caddick • Year 5
Moor Allerton Prep School
Manchester

Jancis Robinson OBE
Wine Critic

A Great Bunch

We're a great bunch
Pinot said to his mates
Full bodied, sun ripe, juicy
Red grapes

Our popularity knows
No end
We seem to be needed
Become the trend

We've hung out together
All season long
We all know what for?
I do hope we're wrong!

We are due to be picked as
September is nigh
I'm a little de-pressed
I think you'll know why!

Dreaming

'Ladies and gentleman *Strictly Come Dancing*'

But LOOK its fruit and vegetables prancing!

The rhubarb rumbas on the floor

The turnips twist by the door

Watermelons waltz beneath the lights

And the can-can carrots wear fishnet tights.

Foxtrotting fennels flash their feet

Whilst raspberry rock and rollers groove to the beat

Sadly this is only a dream

But I know fruit and veg are more fun than they seem!

Emma Mansell • Year 6
The Abbey Junior School
Reading

Blackberries

A tiny seed beneath the ground,
Slowly began to grow,
Its roots pushed down down but made no sound,
The bush grew up so slow.

One bright autumn day in the park,
We saw the berries shining,
Hidden behind the tree trunks bark
Soon we would be dining.

We picked a tonne of glistening fruit,
And saw the purple sheen,
We had to put them in the boot,
And lick our fingers clean.

When we got home we made a pie,
With the greatest pastry,
So delicious it made me sigh,
It was just so tasty!

Rebecca Higginbottom • Year 6
St Pauls Catholic Primary School
Cheshire

Dan Freedman
Author

Fruity Question

Can you please answer me one simple question: How does a fruit know what colour it should be?

After all, every banana knows that it should turn yellow, even though it starts off as green.
And all good plums know that a deep purple is what makes us the most keen.

But what if things were completely different? A surprise to you and me?

What if we woke up one day to find that all the lemons had turned black and all oranges had now decided to be blue?
And just imagine what *that* would do to the colour of your ... tongue!

Eat Your Greens

Vegetables can be orange or green
Or they could be black like aubergine
Some look like icicles or like trees
But my favourite are the small round peas
Some are nice cold
Some are nice hot
Some taste better fresh from the corner shop
I like mine with roast dinners or with a pie
I even like mine in soup
You should try!
Vegetables are good for you
Don't go without
I know some are horrible, like a brussel sprout
Vegetables are one of your five a day
But if you don't eat them
Your health will pay!

Amelia Tranter • Year 6
Heathfield School
Pinner

Ellen's Fruit Bowl Rap

My name is Ellen (Yeah)
And I like my melon (Yeah)
That tasted of lemon (Yeah)
One day I had strawberries
Mixed in with cherries
Then I had grapes (Yeah)
Mixed in with plums
They help me do my sums.
NOW IT'S RAP TIME!
Pineapple and blackberries (Yeah)
Kiwi, oranges and pears,
Gave me lots of energy
Ran up and down the stairs (Yeah)
Banana and tomatoes
Makes my toes grow
Lemon and lime
Help me tell the time (Yeah)
Apples for times tables and
Oranges for my eyes
Blueberries mixed with blackberries
Mean I don't tell lies (Yeah)
I like fruit bowl when its
Time for bed (Yeah)
Makes me bright in the head (Yeah)

Now its time for school
Got to keep the rules (Yeah)
Got to keep my head cool
Dive into a fruit pool (Yeah)
Don't forget that melon
Coz my name is Ellen.

Ellen Brown • Year 6
Meadowdale Primary School
Leicestershire

Lulu Guinness

Fashion Designer

Potato Free Fall

Mr Potato knew there was a catch,
When he was offered a sky dive with no strings attached.

Riding high into the clouds he sweated starch,
His brow was wrinkled, his mouth was parched.

'I think I've made a big mistake!' he cried,
'Today is not the day to die!'
I am destined for greater things,
Sautéed, fried, maybe served with beans.

Why oh why did I have to know,
If fluffy clouds were as cold as snow.

As he hurtled through the air, he knew what lay ahead,
Eyes squeezed shut, he could only dread,
Crashing down to earth – was he dead?

No, creamy and mashed, he'd never looked thinner,
What a delicious treat for someone's dinner!

Five a Day

Oranges, apples, kiwis and dates
Make a fruit salad with a wonderful taste
Corn, broccoli and cauliflower too
All of these veggies are healthy for you
Carrots will help you to see in the dark
Tomatoes and grapes are good for your heart
If your SAT's are causing you strain
Eat some walnuts, they're good for the brain
Have a guava, a strawberry or a lychee
These fruits are rich in vitamin C
Peas, lentils and any kind of bean
Are fortified with lots of protein
The essential vitamins from A to K
Are in fruit and veg. So …
EAT FIVE A DAY!

Andre Morrison • Year 6
St James Primary School
Walsall

Fruit and Veg School

In the school when the lights are out,
The fruit and veg are messing about.
The peas are in detention,
The pears writing a test
The plums are playing football,
With a mango in the net.

The strawberries are at the disco
The ugly fruits playing basketball,
The carrots hanging out,
While his mates are mucking about.

But the best of the lot,
(The apple of course) is writing his socks off
For the Pound a Poem competition!

Alex Beard • Year 6
Bury & Whitefield Jewish Primary School
Bury

Grapes

Grapes grow in colossal clans.

The vine branches curl like little hands,

Cradling the grapes as they bud in the summer sun

Their maroon skin and juicy flesh ripen,

Ready for humans to pick.

Transformed into sweets, juices and wine.

And the vine sleeps in the winter breeze.

Safia Mahmood • Year 6
The Butts Primary School
Hampshire

Stuart Rose
CEO of Marks and Spencer

Cool Cucumber

I am collected and cool
I have been since school.
It's become well accepted,
my coolness, expected.

For me success is not about grades
but about the right car, the right shades:
I drive a green Lotus, neon bright
and wear my Raybans day and night.

The rest of the salad gets continually jealous
that I am so hip, and so zealous
about always maintaining my cool
Tall, thin, icy cool: that's my rule.
But there's a certain amount of pressure

To always look cooler, always seem fresher.
It's a tiresome motivator
to remain as cool as the refrigerator

And I hear them talk about me; how I got no taste
I'm nothing but water, add no inches to the waist.
So you begin to see that my cool exterior
Is really just to stop me feeling inferior

I've got a thick skin, dark tough and green
But don't think I don't feel pain when the lettuces
are mean.
My white flesh is pocked with insecurities and fears
And my seeds down the middle are flecked with my tears

So if my life in this salad bowl has any kind of moral
Nestling amidst the rocket, raddichio and sorrel,
it's this: next time you dismiss someone for being cold
as ice
just think they'd probably warm up if you start being nice.

Ma Veggie Broth

A came hame for ma denner

We were havin veggie broth

A sit at the baird

An fold ma cloth

A pick up ma spuin

And chew doon ma veggies

They slide down ma thrapple

Wi ma tattie wedges

A call tae ma wife

Wifie hand me some mair

She looks in the pan

And fills ma bowl

I am fu o broth

And that's it all

Arran Cottam • Year 6
Westruther Primary School
Scotland

201

John Haynes
Author

On Not Over-Cooking the Vedge

Sometimes when I cook the vedge,
I look across the hedge
and see him, my pretend
caveman friend,
whose name is Harry Hairy,
reaching for a berry

And when the sky gets dim
I chat to him,
he by the windowpane
me standing once again
here at the stove or sink.

We talk a lot
about the small shallot
the cabbage and the colly
this sprout, this broc, this chilli,
these runner beans, this corn
these mushrooms from the lawn.

then plop them in the pot
and heat but not, but not, but not
of course, too long,
because you need the strong
hard crunch of it,
the lovely molar munch of it.

That keeps the iron in,
says Harry, and the vitamin.
I cook the chewy roots
with juicy shoots
and little spikes
that Harry likes
the ones that once he found
under the ground
next to the tree,
so he tells me
so I imagine
cutting the aubergine
here at the window,
draining first the sweet potato
(good for roughage)
then the cabbage.

I whet his appetite
for cabbage stumps he loves to bite

Sometimes he'll get me sheaves
of dandelion leaves
or nettles, even, from the deep
grass by the compost heap.

I'm not much of a cook, no, but
I can still rinse and cut
and bring a pot to boil,
and add a little virgin oil
and salt to taste, and season
with some sage out of the garden,
maybe add a hint
of parsley, thyme or mint,

with those teeth at the back
and carrots he can crack
because they've not been spoiled
by being over boiled.

Although I just pretend
I have a caveman friend
I know
that even so,
the vedges I prepare
will make him melt into the air
or else dissolve among
the jolly juices of my tongue.

Mum's Fruit

Go on, try one, just a bit,

No one else will notice it,

Its red and rosy,

Plump and pure,

With a fat and juicy taste for more,

Through the lips and past the gums,

Watch out tummy, here it comes!

Oh the glory! Oh the taste!

For mum to keep, would be a waste

I'll just have one or maybe two

Oh I could not stop eating you!

4,3,2,1

But where have all the others gone?

Oops!

Molly O'Toole • Year 6
Nether Green Junior School
Sheffield

Mushrooms

Mushrooms
Rich, creamy, golden-coloured table tops,
Like a tasty, sweet, expensive ice cream in the summer.

Mushrooms
Wide and protective, they are guarding gazebos,
Sheltering the insects from rain and shading them in the
sun.

Mushrooms
A sharp snap like someone crunching a crisp,
As a giant hand rips the house off the ground

Mushrooms
Boiling in the pan for a late Sunday breakfast,
Soft, spongy and filling….perfect in your stomach!

Mushrooms
Deliciously warm, filling and satisfying,
Like sitting by the fire on a cold winter's day.

Lizzie Beavis • Year 6
St Paul's Walden School
Hertfordshire

Will Carling OBE
Former England Rugby Player

The Raw and Moody Mushrooms

There was a whole kerfuffle

As Morel and Truffle

Were boiling and feeling wild!

They went into a panic

At becoming organic

They said they'd rather be dried

Oyster lost control

With poor girolles, and

Shitake ended up on the floor

Porcini decreed,

And they all agreed

Pieds Bleus,

Don't eat them

Raw!!

Brian Moses

Poet

Musical Fruit

Imagine fruit that sings to you
before you eat it!

Imagine bananas
bringing you a lilting reggae tune
from the Caribbean

or oranges
rocking and rolling around the room.

Imagine a watermelon
shrieking out some heavy metal

or a plum
whistling a Beethoven symphony.

Grapes could form a choir,
a pair of pears could sing harmony.

Tangerines
could do mean Elvis impersonations
while kiwi fruits do karaoke to Kylie.

Imagine opera
brought to you from the fruit bowl,

...mes, strawberries, raspberries, cherries all making merry
with musicals.

How marvellous it would be
hearing such healthy cacophony!

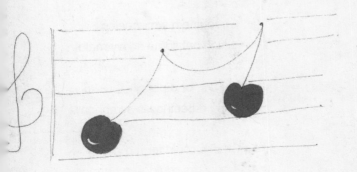

My Fruit Bowl

My fruit bowl is always full
Of colours and interesting shapes
I pick out everyday from there
And eat the goodness and taste the tastes.

My fruit bowl changes shape as the week goes by
It dips in the middle and then fills up to over flow
And its colour does not stay the same.
Now its green and then it's got an orange glow
Soon it will become somewhere in-between.

I love to crunch on crispy apples
Or sometimes I fancy something soft –
A banana or peach will do.
When I am thirsty I go for the tangerines.
Juice bursts into my mouth
And I don't stop at one or two.

Some days my fruit bowl looks different
A new shape of an exotic fruit is there
I want to open it like a present
Will it be green or red?
Dry or wet?
With bits in or smooth?
Really yummy or easy to share?

Maria Hookway • Year 6
Hadley Wood School
London

Paul H. Tubb

Children's Poet

All I am saying

Penny had an octopus,
She fed it bits of cheese,
Sticks of rock and cubes of stock,
But never any peas.
If she tried to feed it peas,
They'd be thrown right back.
With peas coming from 8 directions
Penny couldn't defend the attack.
She tried hiding peas in other foods,
Every once in a while,
But Octopuses have pea sensors
So the attempt was simply futile.
Penny would say, 'They're good for you,
Your health they do enhance.
Listen all I am saying,
Is: 'Give Peas a Chance.'

The Lemon

The electrical buzz on my tongue,
Reminding me of a Caribbean holiday
Bitter, sharp, sour, BANG!
The zingy juice squirting in my mouth as I bite,

The smell is like refreshing soap.
The scent jumping up and down in my nose,
Like a child on a trampoline.

Looking like a yellow luminous light,
The oval shaped fruit, with a pitted rind
Hides a hundred bitter pips.

Cold and waxy, fitting perfectly in my hand.
Moulding as I squeeze,
Nature's acid bomb
.....a LEMON!

Christian Partridge • Year 6
Hunter Hall School
Cumbria

215

Eric Ode
**Songwriter, Author, Poet, Musical Kids' Entertainer
and TV Presenter**

Poor Squash

It's rather sad.
It seems a shame.
It's such an unattractive name.

Squash.
Poor Squash.

It's like a curse.
It's like a joke.
His friends have names
like Artichoke,
and Turnip,
Radish,
Yam,
Tomato,
Rhubarb,
Onion,
Sweet Potato.

And then there's Squash.
Poor Squash.

When they're playing
in the park
and Mother shouts,
'It's getting dark!
Squash! Squash!
Come inside!'
I wonder if
he wants to hide.
I wonder if
he hangs his head
and wishes that
his name was Fred.

The Lettuce

A bush of ruffled leaves,
Overlapping each other,
To capture the flavour inside,
Wig of emerald curls,
Leafy green piece of tissue fluttering,
A Spanish dress covered in all different greens,
Caught in a ball of goodness.

A lettuce!

Amy Brooke • Year 6
St Gerrards Junior School
Wales

The Passion Fruit

Skin as smooth as a summer leaf.
Seeds stick to you like they don't want to let go.
Inside, is as yellow as the sun on a summers day.
Taste is as sweet as a lollypop.
Flesh is huddling up like penguins when it's cold.
Skin guarding the secret treasure like soldiers.
Seeds like thousands of eyes staring into the light.
Squeezing the fruit, sour juice dribbles down like a boat
Floating in the narrow river.
Sweet smell, drifting up into your nostrils like it's attracted
to you.

Carl Mason • Year 6
London Meadow School
Milton Keynes

Wendy Salisbury

Author

The Mint and the Rosemary

(To the tune of The Owl & the Pussycat)

The Mint and the Rosemary went with Pea
To a pot with a snow white goat
They added Lime and a touch of Thyme
All served in a gravy boat.
The Mint looked up to the moon above
And sang to a small sitar
'O lovely Rosem'ry, O Rosem'ry my love
What a tasty young Herb you are
You are!
What a tasty young Herb you are.'

The Potato

It grows under the ground
And it's dirty and brown.
It's not the prettiest vegetable,
It's actually quite forgettable.

But the humble spud
Is really no dud.
For commoners and nobility
It has such versatility.

You can roast it or mash it
Or cook it in its jacket
You can make it into chips
And smother them with dips.

Michael Clark • Year 6
St John's Prep School
Potters Bar

Avocado

The golden pear's ugly sister
Squats fatly in my hand
Skin like the hide of a toad.

Bathed under cerulean skies
The plantation shimmers in ivory heat
Avocadoes adorn undulating trees

I slice it in half, twist gently and pull it apart.
The glossy interior is revealed.
The mahogany stone, like a conker,
Nestles snugly in the buttery jade flesh.
My teaspoon hollows out
Irresistible velvety scoops of pulp
Which dissolve in my mouth.
The nutty, creamy flavour
Makes my tastebuds sing,
As I scoop the last scraps from the skin.

Julia Routledge • Year 6
Port Regis School
Dorset

222

The Winners

Emma Mansell, Winner, 'Dreaming'

Cathal Gilmour, Runner Up, 'The Ugly Fruit'

Ellen Chancellor, Runner Up, 'I Love School Jackets'

Leon Bozianu, Runner Up, 'Apple Tree'

William James Pulle, Runner Up, 'Does Fernando Torres Eat Chillis?'

Julia Routledge, Runner Up, 'Avocado'

About Rays of Sunshine

It is estimated that there are currently 20,000 children across the United Kingdom suffering from life-limiting conditions, many of whom will not live to reach adulthood. For the children, it is a distressing, confusing and uncertain time. Parents may feel unprepared and upset at seeing their child in hospital and siblings often feel left out. To have a wish granted brings so much to a child's life, and provides memories for the family that will last a lifetime.

Rays of Sunshine Children's Charity exists to grant the wishes of children who are living with serious or life-threatening illnesses between the ages of 3-18 in the United Kingdom.

It does this by:
Granting these children's wishes however impossible the wish may seem
Purchasing equipment such as electric wheelchairs or hoists to make their lives easier
Helping hospitals, hospices and specialist schools improve their facilities

Proceeds from this book will enable us to continue granting wishes for terminally and seriously ill children.

Thank you for your support.

Pound a Poem and Rays of Sunshine would like to thank the Barbados Tourism Authority for their generosity and support in donating the wonderful first prize to the competition.

SCHOLASTIC

Pound a Poem and Rays of Sunshine would like to thank the Scholastic for their generosity and support in donating book vouchers to each regional winning school.

To find out more about Rays of Sunshine and Pound a
Poem, visit <u>www.poundapoem.co.uk</u>

Index of Poems (listed by poet)

Celebrity Poems